D1727961

I'M UNDER CONSTRUCTION!!

Story and Coloring Book
"Gods' work on a child from a child's view"

LOREN D. HARRIS

ISBN 978-1-960063-18-2 (softcover)
ISBN 978-1-960063-19-9 (hardcover)
ISBN 978-1-960063-20-5 (ebook)

Printed in the United States of America.

Book Vine Press
2516 Highland Dr.
Palatine, IL 60067

I dedicate this book to my readers who trusted me enough to buy it. Thank You all so very much and please enjoy!

Acknowledgement

I'd like to thank my Lord and Savior Jesus The Christ for giving me the words on these pages. I am nothing without Him. I'm forever grateful to you Lord! Your Word will stand forever!

Preface

This book is directly given by the Holy Spirit to Loren to give her readers a blessed start to their day. The Lord is good to all and His mercy endures forever. Thanks be to God!

I'm under construction
a child with scars

God is working on me like a mechanic on a car!

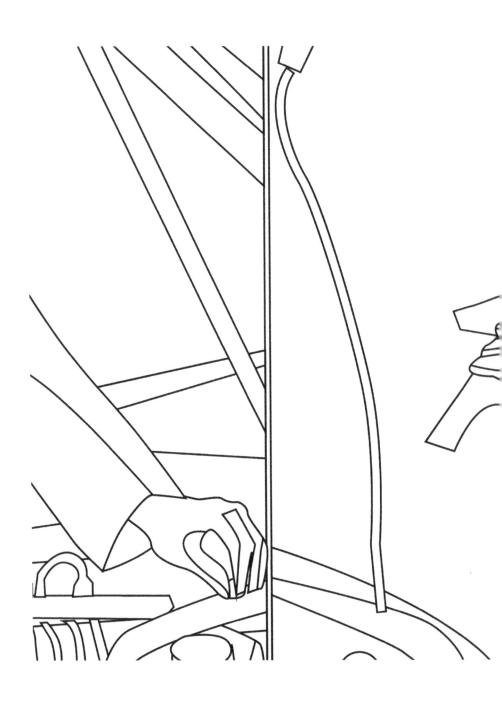

He's molding, shaping and making me brand new!

Don't give up on me because He's still not through!

I'm under construction,
by God and not man

No one will get the Glory, as only God can

God is creator and maker of all,
He created man and woman before the great fall!

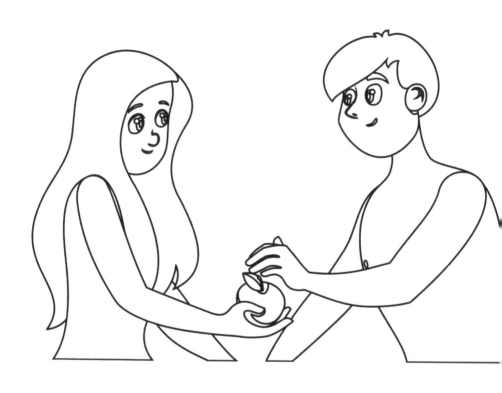

I'm under construction,
with plenty of nailing,

Keep me in your prayers,
because the devil wants me failing!

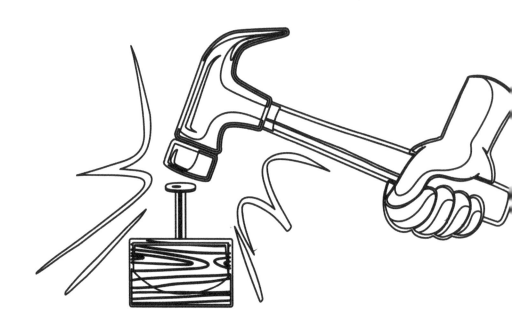

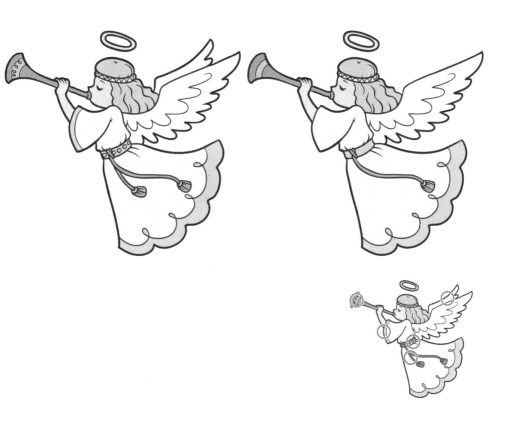

Let all of heaven and earth proclaim,

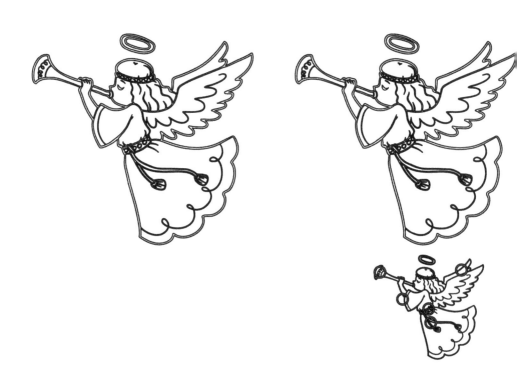

When God is finished with me there
will be no shame!

God is still working on me
and even on you!

creative people

CONSTRUCTION #1
build your own world

"We" are under construction,
and "not" by the motley crew!

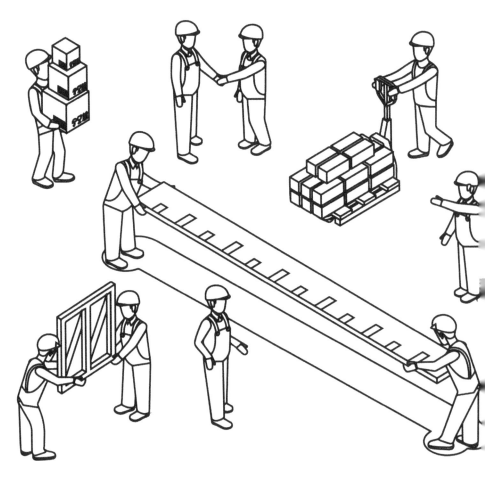

CONSTRUCTION #1
build your own world

God created me with others in mind,
I am here for a purpose to be a blessing to mankind!

In God's hands are a chisel,
drill and a saw,
He's chipping away things that will make me fall.

I'm under construction,
being made brand new,

While my building is being completed,
I'll be there for you!

So don't let it surprise you how I run this race,
My building has some
repairing that is taking place!

The builder and maker is the best around,
When this building is finished
it won't fall to the ground!

Because, I'm Under construction!!!

About the Author

The Author, Loren Harris is a wife, Minister, avid reader and Executive Assistant, who lives in NJ with her husband of 42 years. She attends a large church congregation in New Jersey. She loves the Lord and loves writing about Him. She has published a Christian poetry book called "Poetry from the Heart, Joy for the Soul", a children's book called "I'm Under Construction" and is currently working on the 3rd of 4 quarterly daily devotionals named the same as this book, which will be on Amazon, Barnes and Noble and Walmart.com very soon.

CPSIA information can be obtained
at www.ICGtesting.com
Printed in the USA
BVHW011133130123
656257BV00005B/277